Animals Around the World

All About North American Bison

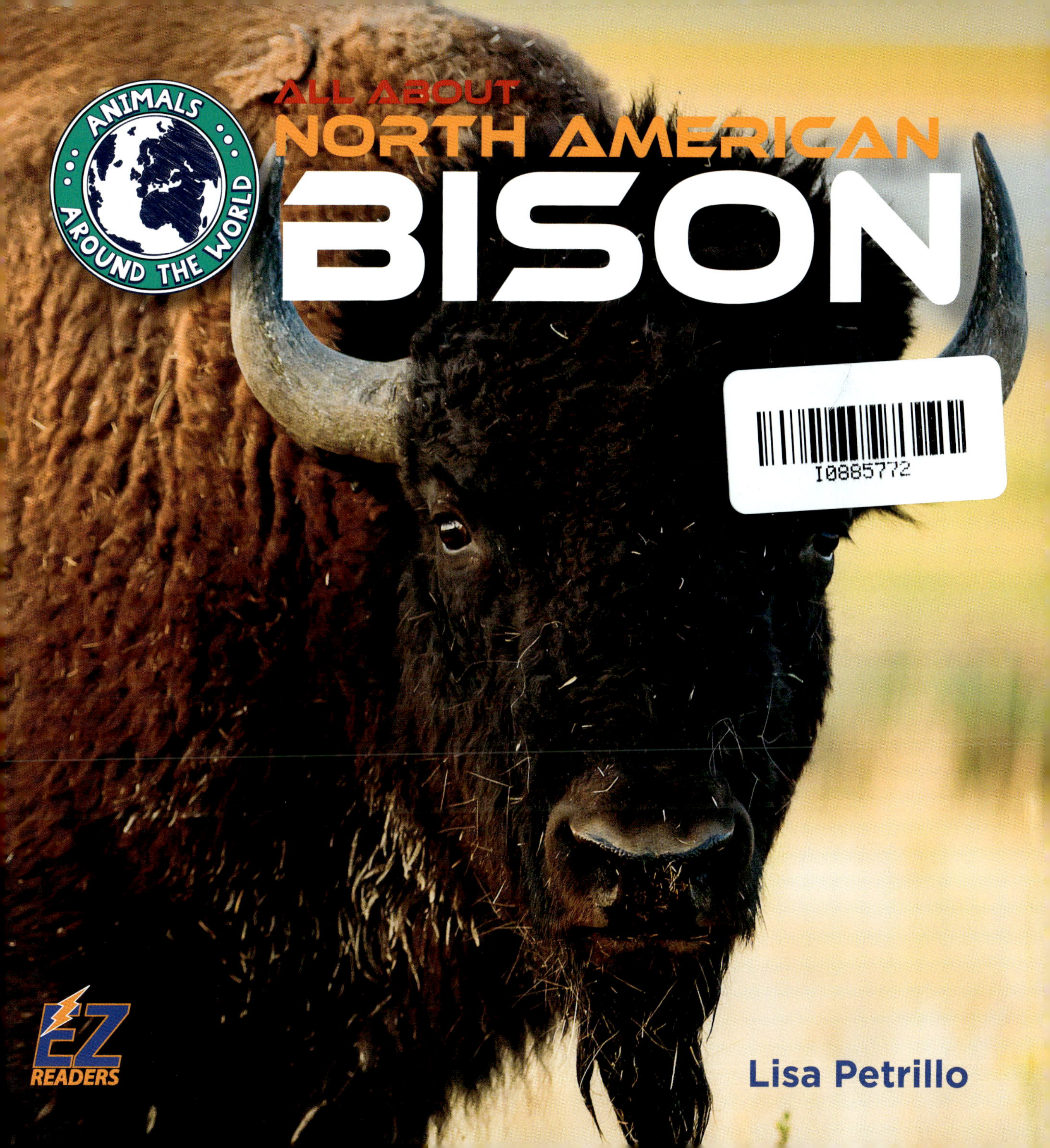

EZ Readers

Lisa Petrillo

Creating Young Nonfiction Readers

EZ Readers lets children delve into nonfiction at beginning reading levels. Young readers are introduced to new concepts, facts, ideas, and vocabulary.

Tips for Reading Nonfiction with Beginning Readers

Talk about Nonfiction
Begin by explaining that nonfiction books give us information that is true. The book will be organized around a specific topic or idea, and we may learn new facts through reading.

Look at the Parts
Most nonfiction books have helpful features. Our *EZ Readers* include a Contents page, an index, and color photographs. Share the purpose of these features with your reader.

Contents
Located at the front of a book, the Contents displays a list of the big ideas within the book and where to find them.

Index
An index is an alphabetical list of topics and the page numbers where they are found.

Glossary
Located at the back of the book, a glossary contains key words/phrases that are related to the topic.

Photos/Charts
A lot of information can be found by "reading" the charts and photos found within nonfiction text. Help your reader learn more about the different ways information can be displayed.

With a little help and guidance about reading nonfiction, you can feel good about introducing a young reader to the world of *EZ Readers* nonfiction books.

Mitchell Lane
PUBLISHERS

2001 SW 31st Avenue
Hallandale, FL 33009
www.mitchelllanepub.com

First Edition, 2025.

Author: Lisa Petrillo
Designer: Ed Morgan
Editor: Sharon F. Doorasamy

Names/credits:
Title: All About North American Bison / by Lisa Petrillo
Description: Hallandale, FL : Mitchell Lane Publishers, [2025]

Series: Animals Around the World
Library bound ISBN: 9781680204155
eBook ISBN: 9781680204162
Paperback ISBN: 9798892601344

EZ readers is an imprint of Mitchell Lane Publishers

Library of Congress Cataloging-in-Publication Data
Names: Petrillo, Lisa, author.
Title: All about North American bison / by Lisa Petrillo.
Description: First edition. | Hallandale, FL : EZ Readers, an imprint of Mitchell Lane Publishers, 2020. | Series: Animals around the world-North American animals | Includes bibliographical references and index.
Identifiers: LCCN 2018030962| ISBN 9781680204155 (library bound) | ISBN 9781680204162 (ebook)
Subjects: LCSH: American bison—Juvenile literature.
Classification: LCC QL737.U53 P44 2020 | DDC 599.64/3—dc23
LC record available at https://lccn.loc.gov/2018030962

Photo credits: Freepik.com, Shutterstock.com, mapchart.netmapchart.net

CONTENTS

Bison are **mammals**. Wild bison live in national parks.

Bison are brown. They grow fur to stay warm. They shed their coats in spring.

They eat grass and plants.

Bison have humps like camels.

A bison's horns are sharp. Male bison are **bulls**. Females are **cows**. Baby bison are **calves**.

Calves walk soon after being born. They stay with their mothers for two years. This helps to keep them safe. Wolves and coyotes steal baby calves.

Bison stand for strength and freedom. They are the national mammal of the United States.

WHERE DO BISON LIVE?

Yellowstone National Park is the best place to see wild herds of bison. About 5,000 roam there.

INTERESTING FACTS

- Buffalo are animals that are related to the bison but live in Asia and Africa.
- They live for up to 25 years in the wild.
- Bison can run as fast as a car traveling 35 miles per hour.
- Bison stand as tall as college basketball players, at 6-foot-5 inches.
- Bison were the most important animal to many Native Americans. They used the bison for food, tools, clothing, medicine, tents, and toys.

PARTS OF A BISON

Eyes
Bison have poor eyesight.

Hump
The backbone above the head of a bison rises into a hump like a camel.

Hooves
The feet of bison are similar to cattle.

Tail
The bison tail is long with a tuft, or clump of hair, at the end.

Fur
Bison fur grows shaggy in winter to keep them warm. In spring they roll around in the dirt to rub off the extra fur.

Skin
The hide of bison is turned into leather goods such as wallets, boots, shoes, travel bags, and pants.

GLOSSARY

buffalo
What some people call bison

calves
Young bison

cow
Female bison

bull
Male bison

mammal
A warm-blooded animal that breathes air, has a backbone, and drinks its mother's milk when a baby

FURTHER READING

Perry, Phyllis J. *Buffalo*. New York: Marshall Cavenish, 2006.

Potts, Steve. *American Bison*. North Mankato, MN: Capstone Press, 2012.

"15 Facts About Our National Mammal: The American Bison." Blog. The U.S. Department of the Interior. https://www.doi.gov/blog/15-facts-about-our-national-mammal-american-bison.

ON THE INTERNET

"How Many Ways Can You Use a Buffalo?" Texas Beyond History. The Virtual Museum of Texas' Cultural History.
https://www.texasbeyondhistory.net/kids/buffalo.html

"Bison." Yellowstone National Park. National Park Service.
https://www.nps.gov/yell/learn/nature/bison.htm

INDEX